TERMS & CONDITIONS

No part of this physical book can be transmitted or reproduced in any form, including photocopying, electronic, print, scanning, recording or mechanical without prior written permission of the author. All information, ideas, & guidelines are for educational purpose only. Though the author has tried to ensure the utmost accuracy of content, all readers are advised to follow instructions at their risk. The author of this book cannot be held liable for any incidental damage, personal or commercial caused by misrepresentation of information. Readers are encouraged to seek professional help when needed

TABLE OF CONTENTS

Chapter 1 – Juice Recipes

Now I can go on telling the benefits of juices but you probably know them already. They are healthy, better than cold drinks and just amazing.

I know you already know that. Let's check the recipes straightaway.

Epic Blackberry Grape

Just make it once and you will keep making it!!

Ingredients

- Two-three cups fresh red grapes
- 1/2 - 1 cup fresh blackberries

The method of preparation

1. Assemble all the ingredients at one place.
2. Now wash the fruit thoroughly.
3. Now we may proceed to the following most important step.
4. Withdraw stems.

5. One thing remains to be done now.
6. Now please place all the ingredients into your juicer and then process them.
7. Now you can serve immediately.
8. Smell the aroma and now serve.

Servings: 1 - 2 glass.

Nutrition Facts:

Calories from Fat 9.687

Total Fat 1.15g

Monounsaturated Fat 0.0275g

Polyunsaturated Fat 0.2456g

Sugars 4.985g

Protein 2.475g

Sodium 6.15mg

Potassium 468.75mg

Calories 74.25

Saturated Fat 0.029g

Total Carbohydrate 37.26g

Duke Cabbage Berry Juice

Royal taste…

What you need:

- 1 - 2 cucumber
- One red apple
- One pinch of cinnamon
- 1/4 - 1/2 red cabbage
- 1/2 - 1 cup fresh raspberries
- 1/2 cup fresh blueberries

Directions:

1. Assemble all the ingredients at one place.
2. Process cabbage, cucumber, raspberries, blueberries and apple through a juicer.
3. One thing remains to be done now.

4. Stir the resulting juice, and now you should add the cinnamon.
5. Serve.
6. Go ahead and enjoy!!

Servings: 2-4

Preparation Time: 13 minutes

I used to go to my amazing & awesome neighbor's house to eat this one.

Nutritional Info: Protein 3.15 g, Calories 82.25, Fat .725 g, Carbs 32.25 g

Cute Cancun

Sincere efforts will be awesome.

Ingredients

- Six-seven leaves kale
- 1-2 cucumber
- One lime
- ½ -1 small handful mint
- One jalapeño
- Two-three ribs celery

Directions:

1. Assemble all the ingredients at one place.
2. Peel lime.
3. Now we can proceed to the next most important step.
4. Withdraw seeds from jalapeño.

5. One thing remains to be done now.
6. Wash all ingredients.
7. Now please add all ingredients through your juicer and just enjoy!
8. Go ahead and enjoy!!

Servings: 1 to 2

Just wonder about an excellent, excellent and delicious recipe that it just a treat for your tongue and tummy. The wait is over.

Nutritional Info:

Calories   : 78.15 / 676.25kJ

Fat: 3.15g

Sodium: 3.15mg

Carbohydrate: 28.25g

Sugars: 5.95g

Protein: 7.65g

Legendary Apple pear and spinach juice

We all are legends in some ways.

Ingredients

- 4-5 fresh mint sprigs
- Four Ice cubes and mint sprigs to serve immediately
- 140 to 145g baby spinach
- 3-4 large Packham pears
- Two-three large granny smith apples

What to do

1. Assemble all the ingredients at one place.
2. Put a large jug under juice extractor nozzle.

3. Juice the pear, mint, spinach, apple using a juicer.
4. Now we may proceed to the next most important step.
5. Divide ice cubes between chilled glasses.
6. One thing remains to be done now.
7. Top with pear juice mixture then serve it with mint.
8. For this preparation, you need a juice extractor.
9. Smell the aroma and now serve.

Perfect start of the day; it is one of the rarest recipes.

Stunning Turbo Boost

I remember the time I learned this recipe. It was just an excellent, exceptional recipe.

Ingredients

- 5-6 Ounces of Water
- 4-5 Cherries
- 8-9 Strawberries

How to make:

1. Assemble all the ingredients at one place.
2. Prepare your strawberries by washing them.
3. One thing remains to be done now.
4. Combine the cherries & strawberries in your juicer,

and now you should add the
water.

5. Blend the ingredients
together for at least thirty to
forty seconds and enjoy!

6. Smell the aroma, and now
you may serve.

Make it quickly.

Refrshing Strawberry, Blueberry & Apple Combo

Refreshing

Ingredients

- 1-2 apple, cored
- 1-2 cup blueberries
- Four-five strawberries

Directions

1. Assemble all the ingredients at one place.
2. Now wash the fruit thoroughly.
3. One thing remains to be done now.
4. Now please place all the ingredients into your juicer and just process them.

5. Serve immediately.
6. Smell the aroma and serve.

Servings: 1 - 2 glass.

Silently waiting…

Nutrition Facts

Calories: 114.25

Calories from Fat: 5.69

Total Fat: 0.615g

Saturated Fat: 0.0635g

Cholesterol: 1.15mg

Sodium: 5mg

Potassium: 251mg

Total Carbohydrate: 34.45g

Dietary Fiber: 0.3g

Sugars: 24.77g

Protein: 1.225g

Stunning Ginger, Coconut & Watermelon Juice Combo

Astonishing!!

Ingredients:

- One-Two cups coconut water
- 1 - 2 lemons
- One pinch of ginger powder
- One handful mint leaves
- 1 - 2 cucumber
- Two cups watermelon
- Two-three tablespoons honey

Directions:

1. Assemble all the ingredients at one place.

2. Cut the watermelon and the cucumber roughly.
3. Juice the watermelon and the cucumber together with the mint leaves.
4. Now we can proceed to the next most important step.
5. Place the resulting juice into a blender and combine the rest of the ingredients.
6. One thing remains to be done now.
7. Blend until the juice is smooth.
8. Now you can serve.
9. Go ahead and enjoy!!

Classic style…

Servings: Two-three

Prep Time: Thirteen minutes

Nutritional Info: Calories 215, Fat 0 g, Protein 8 g, Carbs 53 g

Historic Green Juice

Ingredients:

- 1 - 2 cup spinach¨
- Half-Two tsp spirulina
- 1/2 - 2 stalks celery
- 2 - 3 Apples
- 1 - 2 cups kale

Instructions

1. Assemble all the ingredients at one place.
2. Withdraw core from the apple.
3. Now wash all the fruits and veggies.
4. Now we can proceed to the next most important step.

5. Juice the fruits and veggies and then stir to smooth out consistency and taste.
6. One thing remains to be done now.
7. Whisk in or blend with the spirulina
8. Serve or chill in the refrigerator.
9. Go ahead and enjoy!!

Always the upper hand…

Servings: 1-2

Prep Time: 14 minutes

Nutritional Info: Calories: 164.25, Protein 2.55 g, Carbs 27.25

Lucky Carrot, beetroot & celery

Now you're happy…?

Ingredients

- Two peeled oranges
- 1-2 carrots
- 1-2 cm slice of ginger
- One-Two small beetroot
- ½ -1 celery stick
- 2 apples

The method of preparation

1. Assemble all the ingredients at one place.
2. Chill the ingredients
3. One thing remains to be done now.
4. Now please feed the vegetables & fruits through

your juice maker and then
pour crushed ice above it.
5. Serve it immediately.
6. Go ahead and enjoy!!

Mystical Minty Beet, Carrots, and Apple Juice

Prepare yourself for this…

Ingredients:

- One small beet
- 4-5 carrots
- ¼-1/2 cup fresh mint sprigs
- 1-2 apple

The method of preparation:

1. Assemble all the ingredients at one place.
2. Remove apple cored and cut beet, carrots and apple.
3. One thing remains to be done now.

4. Drop ingredients within the juicer including the fresh mint sprigs.
5. Juice the ingredients, whisk then serve.
6. Go ahead and enjoy!!

Looking forward to healthy life.

Preparation Time: 7 to 8 minutes

Ready In: 6 to 7 minutes

Servings: 1 - 2

Extraordinary Strawberry, Maca & Banana Juice Combo
You're lucky

What you need:

- ½ -1 teaspoon Maca powder
- 1-2 tsp honey
- Two-three tsp beet extract
- 1-2 banana
- ½ cup strawberries
- 1-2 lemon

Directions:

1. Assemble all the ingredients at one place.
2. Wash the strawberries and withdraw their leafy heads.

3. Place the lemon and strawberries within your juicer.
4. Now we can proceed to the next most important step.
5. Place the resulting juice into a blender, and now you should add the rest of the ingredients.
6. One thing remains to be done now.
7. Blend for a few seconds until the juice is smooth.
8. Now you can serve.
9. Smell the aroma and now serve.

Servings: 1 - 2

Preparation Time: 13 to 18 minutes

Nutritional Info: Calories 247.25, Protein 7.15 g, Carbs 62.25 g

There it is.

Extra Awesome Green Juice

What you need

- 2-3 ribs celery
- ½ -1 cucumber
- 2 apples
- 2-3 handfuls spinach
- 1-2 carrots

The method of preparation:

1. Assemble all the ingredients at one place.
2. Wash all ingredients.
3. Combine all ingredients through a juicer and enjoy!
4. Go ahead and enjoy!!

Servings: 2 to 4

Magical, isn't it?

Nutritional Info:

Cholesterol: 0.001g

Sodium: 87.25mg

Calories   112.25 / 439.5kJ

Sugars: 16.15g

Protein: 1.18g

Trans Fat: 1.15g

Carbohydrate: 22.21g

Legendary Coconut mango froojie

Ingredients

- 1-2 teaspoon of vanilla extract
- ¼ cup of oat
- 2-3 teaspoon of vanilla extract
- 1-2 mango, peeled and seed removed
- 1-2 teaspoon of ground cardamom
- Coconut

Instructions

1 Assemble all the ingredients at one place.

2 Crack the coconut with a cleaver or a knife.
3 Pour the milk into a jug and set it aside.
4 Now we can proceed to the next most important step.
5 Scoop out the soft flesh.
6 Process the mango and coconut flesh at low speed using a fountain juicer.
7 One thing remains to be done now.
8 Add the vanilla cardamom, and maple syrup or honey, coconut milk to the jug and stir well to mix.
9 Pour into chilled glasses to serve.
10 Go ahead and enjoy!!

Funny Romaine, Chard & Turmeric Juice

Grab it!!

What you need:

- 1-2 small head romaine
- 1-2 oranges, peeled
- One large stalk chard
- 3-4 stalks celery
- ½-1 teaspoon
- One small bunch mint
- 1-2 large cucumber
- 1-2 piece Turmeric root
- ½ - 1 lime

How to prepare:

1 Assemble all the ingredients at one place.

2 Now prepare all ingredients and place all into your juicer one at a time.
3 One thing remains to be done now.
4 Juice it and shift into a serving glass or a container
5 Whisk the juice before serving.
6 Go ahead and enjoy!!

Prep Time: 4 minutes

Ready In: 6 minutes

Servings: 2 - 3

Iconic Pineapple Green Awesome!!

What you need:

- 1-2 1/2 cucumber, cubed or may be cut into pieces small enough to easily fit in the juicer
- Half-One cup coconut water
- 1-2 cups cubed pineapple
- 2-3 cups spinach

The method of preparation:

1 Assemble all the ingredients at one place.
2 Wash the vegetables.
3 Now we can proceed to the next most important step.

4 Juice the pineapple, spinach, and cucumber.
5 One thing remains to be done now.
6 Stir in the coconut water.
7 Now you can serve chilled or maybe with a bit of ice if desired.
8 Go ahead and enjoy!!

Servings: 1 - 2

Preparation time: 15 minutes

Nutritional Info: Calories: 185.15 Fat 1.15 g, Protein 1.35 g Carbs 35.25

Supreme Pink Lemonade

Freshness loaded!!

What you need

- One-Two tbsp of caster sugar extra
- 53g of fresh raspberries or maybe frozen raspberries
- 1-2 lemon
- Raspberry puree
- Fresh mint leaves to garnish
- ½ - 1 cup of caster sugar
- Two-three cups of water
- 365ml of lemon juice
- 1-2 lemon, sliced to garnish

What to do

1 Assemble all the ingredients at one place.

2 Whisk the lemon juice, caster sugar & water in a saucepan over a low heat for 7 minutes or so or when the sugar fully dissolves.

3 Leave it to cool and then chill it for an hour.

4 Now prepare the rasp berry puree by combining the raspberries & extra caster sugar in a saucepan above a low heat.

5 Now we can proceed to the next most important step.

6 Cook it while stirring to lightly crush for approximately four minutes or so or when the sugar dissolves fully and the raspberries breakdown and

release the juices then strain it through a fine sieve into a bowl.

7 Place the lemonade in a serving jug.

8 Add two tablespoon of the raspberry puree and whisk it to mix.

9 Combine sliced lemon, mint leaves & ice cubes to the lemonade.

10 One thing remains to be done now.

11 Divide the left raspberry puree among serving glasses.

12 Sprinkle it with the pink lemonade and now you can serve.

13 Go ahead and enjoy!!

Love it!!

Rich Green Smoothies

Rich taste is always classic.

Ingredients:

- 1-2 mint sprig
- One green apple ,cored, coarsely shredded
- Extra mints prigs to serve immediately
- Lime wedges to serve immediately
- One-two cm piece fresh ginger, peeled and chopped
- 1-2 Lebanese cucumber
- 345ml of coconut water
- 2-3 kale leaves, centre, stem removed
- 1-2 lime, peeled, coarsely shredded

The method of preparation

1 Assemble all the ingredients at one place.
2 Place the kale, ginger, apple, mint, lime, cucumber and coconut water in a blender and blend it until very smooth.
3 Serve in serving glasses with extra lime and mint to make it tasty.
4 Smell the aroma and now serve.

Oh yeah!!

Wild Juice

Wait, what??

Ingredients

- Two-three cups of orange juice
- ¼-1 cup lime-favoured cordial
- 750 to 770ml bottle of soda water
- 750 to 770g pineapple, peeled , cut into 2cm cubes

Method of preparation

1 Assemble all the ingredients at one place.
2 Place the pineapples in a serving jug.
3 One thing remains to be done now.

4 Add soda, orange juice and
   cordial.
5 Stir well to mix, and now
   you can serve.
6 Smell the aroma, and now
   you can serve.

Jungle rules..

Dreamy Orange, Carrot & Coriander Combo

Dreams are good!! So dream about this one or else make it…

What you need

- ½ -1 green apple
- Two-three Corriander sprigs with roots and washed
- 2-3 large carrots
- 2-3 peeled oranges

Instructions

1 Assemble all the ingredients at one place.
2 Process the oranges, carrots, apple & coriander using a froojie fountain juicer.

3 Serve in glasses.
4 Smell the aroma and now serve.

Stupidly simple!!

Cute Pineapple, Lychee & Papaya Combo

Super combo.

Ingredients

- 1-2 papaya (approximately 1 to 1.5 kg), halved, deseeded, peeled & chopped
- 520 to 550ml of pineapple juice
- 1x420g packet of sliced pineapple, cored, quartered & chopped
- 2x585g cans of lychees (undrained)

What to do

1 Assemble all the ingredients at one place.

2 Place half of each of the
  lychees, pineapple, papaya
  and pineapple juice in the
  jug of a blender and the
  blend it until smooth.
3 Transfer it to a jug, now
  repeat it with the leftover
  ingredients and place it in a
  fridge for about 3 hrs.
4 Go ahead and enjoy!!

Fantasy Juice Remake

Something is definitely different.

Ingredients

- Two-three celery stalks
- Two small lemons
- One half-Two cups of water
- 1 - 2 carrot
- Half-One medium beetroot, trimmed & peeled
- One-Two stalks of kale
- Two-three cm piece fresh ginger

What to do

1 Assemble all the ingredients at one place.

2   Remove and discard the stems from kales the roughly cut the leaves.
3   One thing remains to be done now.
4   Now please place all ingredients you have in a blender or mixer and then blend it until smooth.
5   Pour it into glasses and serve immediately.
6   Go ahead and enjoy!!

Exciting!!

Funny Strawberry & Apple Juice Combo

Ingredients

- 1-2 Ice cubes
- ½ -1 large red apple
- 240 To 260g strawberries

What to do

1 Assemble all the ingredients at one place.
2 Now cut the red apple into half and withdraw the core.
3 Now cut each and every of the halves into four wedges.
4 Now we may proceed to the next most important step.
5 Wash the 240 to 260g strawberries and remove the hulls.

6 One thing remains to be
   done now.
7 Process the fruit pieces in a
   juice extractor or blender.
8 Now pour it above ice
   cubes in glasses and serve it
   instantly.
9 Smell the aroma and now
   serve.

It is very easy and quick recipe.

Epic Tomato and celery juice

This is epic. Take a look!!

Ingredients

- ½-1 teaspoon Worcestershire sauce
- 1/2 - 1 celery stick with leaves, chopped
- 320 to 340ml of tomato juice

Instructions

1. Assemble all the ingredients at one place.
2. Using a juice extractor, extract the celery and pour it into a glass.

3. Add the tomato juice and sauce then stir well and now it is ready to be served.
4. Go ahead and enjoy!!

Stunning Strawberry, Vanilla & Orange Juice

LOL!!

Ingredients

- ½ - 1 Juice of lemon
- 4-5 peeled oranges
- 1-2 teaspoon vanilla extract
- 230 to 240g punnet strawberries

Instructions:

1. Assemble all the ingredients at one place.
2. Pass the strawberries and oranges through a juicer, and then transfer it into a jug.
3. One thing remains to be done now.

4. Now you should add lemon juice & vanilla.
5. Whisk it well and it's ready to now you can serve.
6. Smell the aroma and serve.

Hi, thanks for reading my book. I would really love & appreciate if you could leave a review on my book.

Regards

Garry